J
591.92
Whi

DATE DUE

JUN 19 1975	OCT. 18 1984	DE 26'90
FEB 28 1976	JE 17'85	MR 29'91
MAR 8 1976	MY 13'86	JE 5'91
MAY 17 1977	JY 14'86	JY 25'91
SEP 16 1978	OC 22'86	SE 20'91
JUN 18 1979	MY 21'87	OC 29'91
	JE 3'87	MR 9'92
JUL 25 1979		MY 23'92
OCT. 7 1980	AP 2'88	JY 17'92
JUN 22 1981	JY 22'88	AG 9'93
JUL 16 1981	AG 21'88	AUG 15 '94
APR. 12 1982	OC 5'89	OCT 17 '94
	AP 6'90	OCT 01 '95
SEP. 15 1982	MY 14'90	FEB 05 '96
MAY 25 1983		MAR 8 '98
JUN. 28 1983	NO 15'90	JE 26 '00

44,541

White, William, 1934-
    A turtle is born.   N.Y., Sterling, [1973]
96p.   illus.

1.Turtles.   I.Title.

a turtle is born

by William White, Jr., Ph.D.
photographs by the author

STERLING NATURE SERIES

STERLING PUBLISHING CO., INC. NEW YORK

Oak Tree Press Co., Ltd. London & Sydney

STERLING NATURE SERIES

Acknowledgments
The author and publisher wish to thank Mr. Kevin Bowler of the Philadelphia Zoological Garden for his co-operation in the preparation of this book, and Detective Paul Counsellor, Ocean City, New Jersey, for the use of the photographs on pages 80, 81, 82 and 83.

Second Printing, 1974
Copyright © 1973 by Sterling Publishing Co., Inc.
419 Park Avenue South, New York, N.Y. 10016
British edition published by Oak Tree Press Co., Ltd., Nassau, Bahamas
Distributed in Australia and New Zealand by Oak Tree Press Co., Ltd.,
P.O. Box J34, Brickfield Hill, Sydney 2000, N.S.W.
Distributed in the United Kingdom and elsewhere in the British Commonwealth
by Ward Lock Ltd., 116 Baker Street, London W 1
Manufactured in the United States of America
All rights reserved
Library of Congress Catalog Card No.: 72-95220
Sterling ISBN 0-8069-3528-6 Trade   Oak Tree 7061-2437-5
3529-4 Library

CONTENTS

Illus. 1. A turtle's world.

INTRODUCTION

Men have watched and wondered at tortoises and turtles since history began. The silent, slow lives of these animals within the safety of their shells and their long life-spans have fascinated civilized philosophers and primitive tribesmen, as well as artists and soldiers. Aesop, the Greek storyteller, showed how the tortoise by its steady plodding beat the swift hare in a race. The Roman generals used the Latin name *testudo*, or "tortoise," to describe their close defensive formation of troops with shields overlapping like a turtle's shell. When the French ruler, Napoleon Bonaparte, was sent into exile on the desolate island of St. Helena, he took with him a tortoise which lived on after him for nearly a century. The 18th-century American inventor, David Bushnell, called his submarine the "Turtle."

Tortoises and turtles form a well defined branch of the reptile family, the *chelonians*. Properly a tortoise is a land or fresh-water chelonian, while a turtle is a marine form with limbs modified into flippers. In England the distinction between these two terms is

Illus. 2. Ancient extinct land turtle from Southeast Asia.

observed, but in the United States, turtle is the usual word in popular usage for any chelonian. However, some American land species are called commonly tortoises, such as the common box tortoise.

The "shell," or protective shield, is properly called a *carapace*, and is present in all chelonians, although in some it is greatly reduced and modified. In internal structure and body chemistry, tortoises show resemblances to both amphibians and birds.

All tortoises have strong necks and beaks but none have teeth, and all hatch from eggs. Their special structure has stood them in good stead, for they have lumbered across the land and swum in the seas for millions of years. Most of the 250 or more species of chelonians are less than a foot in length. But this was not always so. Millions of years ago great tortoises weighing over a ton and the size of a small motor-car grazed on green plants in Southeast Asia (Illus. 2).

Most of the world's turtles belong to two large groups. One is the *Cryptodira*, consisting of those genera which can withdraw their heads within their shells, and the other is the *Pleurodira*, consisting of those which wrap their heads tightly against their shells, sometimes called the "side-necked" varieties. The soft-shelled turtles form a third, smaller group, and the fourth group consists of a single species, the leathery turtle.

THE LIFE CYCLE
OF THE TURTLE

The chelonians belong to a very large group of animals called by scientists *poikilotherms*, or, more popularly, cold-blooded animals. Unlike birds and mammals, cold-blooded animals cannot regulate heat inside their bodies and so take on the temperature of the outside air, earth, or water where they are found. As a result, the turtle cannot survive in an environment which is too hot or too cold. It will dry out and die of heat, or freeze to death in cold.

In the temperate areas of the world, the turtle's activity is dictated by the round of the seasons. Through internal changes in its chemistry, turtles survive the colder seasons of their range by *hibernation* and the hot-dry seasons by *estivation*. Both of these processes involve the lowering of the turtle's metabolism, something like slowing down a clock, so that it will run longer but slower on one winding.

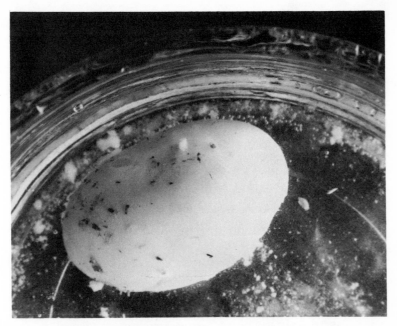

Illus. 3. A medium-sized turtle egg (magnified 3 times).

All of the world's turtles begin life as eggs buried in sand, or in the decaying vegetable matter of forest floors, or in earth. The size of an individual turtle egg depends upon the species and to some extent the size of the female which laid it. Generally, the smallest turtle eggs are about one half inch in diameter and slightly oblong or elliptical in shape. The largest eggs laid by sea turtles are two and a half inches in diameter. Turtle eggs vary in volume from about the size of a small marble (Illus. 3) to about that of a tennis ball.

The egg is usually white—since it is buried, it needs no protective coloration like the eggs of birds or snakes. Most of the eggs are leathery to the touch and covered by a tough fibrous substance that has been secreted by the female. Some species encrust their eggs with calcium, and these appear more like bird's eggs. There is some evidence that sea turtle embryos absorb this calcium in making their own carapaces as they grow towards hatching.

Turtle eggs adsorb water from the surrounding soil and excrete nitrogen-bearing compounds through microscopic pores in the shell. The shell and the egg have very complex structures. These are mostly for the purpose of exchanging gases (a process called respiration) by which the foodstuff, in this case yolk, is oxidized and its energy used up by the embryo for growth.

The turtle's egg is about one half albumen, the substance which we call the "white" in a chicken's eggs. The yellowish yolk is made up of fat and protein, chiefly a substance called *lipo-protein*. The yolk also contains calcium, phosphorus, and trace amounts (tiny amounts) of other minerals, all of which are vital to the growth of the cells which will develop into a turtle. Unlike frogs, turtles are capable of internal fertilization, so the eggs are fertile long before they are actually released. Therefore, the turtle embryo has

Illus. 4. Live turtle eggs inside an incubator.

usually passed through its earliest development before
it leaves the body of the female.

The embryo is attached to the yolk and the albumen
by a series of membranes or sacs. However, the
components or parts of the egg are not as firmly
attached to each other as are the components of a
bird's egg. For this reason, turtle eggs may be damaged
if they are turned over or up-ended, which is not
usually the case with birds' eggs. When turtle eggs
are incubated in zoos or animal farms they are kept in
large sand-filled clay pots (Illus. 4) with moisture-
proof glass covers to preserve heat and water.

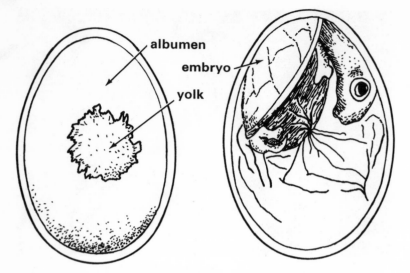

albumen

embryo

yolk

Illus. 5. Diagram of a turtle egg.

The turtle egg (Illus. 5) is a complete nursery, shelter, and food supply in miniature. The embryo usually lies on the top of the matter inside the shell. The first sign of life (to the unaided eye) is the mass of thin red blood vessels called the *vitelline* circulatory system. The embryo releases an enzyme which digests the yolk chemicals; this foodstuff is carried back to it by these vessels. It is not until about the third week after laying that truly turtle-like features start to appear in the embryo. In 60 to 90 days, the egg will twist and bulge with the growing turtle until final hatching nears (Illus. 6).

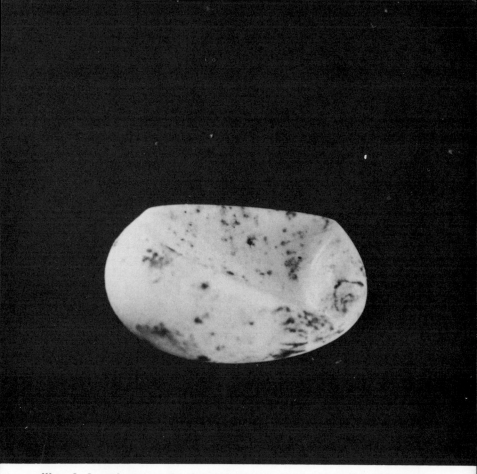

Illus. 6. A turtle egg at the time it begins to twist and turn as hatching approaches.

The backbone, nerves, and circulatory system of the embryo form before the external parts. It is still difficult to make out the head, body and limb buds but they are growing rapidly. Soon the earliest signs

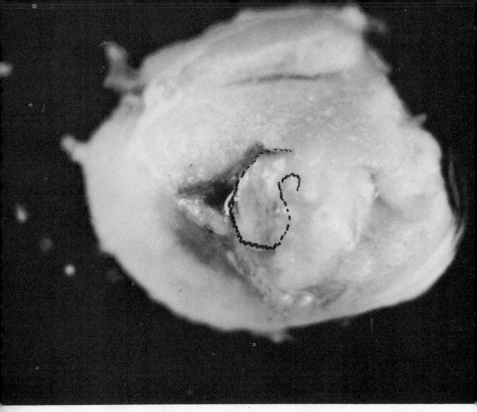

Illus. 7. Embryo in 10-15-mm stage (shell removed). The head is shown in outline.

of the upper shell, or carapace, appear (Illus. 7). When the embryo has reached a length of 15 mm (millimetres) the head starts to grow and soon is nearly as big as the body. The shoulder and hip bones are growing out of the spine, with the ribs along the sides. However, soon the carapace will overtake and fuse to the ribs, shoulders and hips almost as though the embryo were wrapping itself into a box (Illus. 8).

14

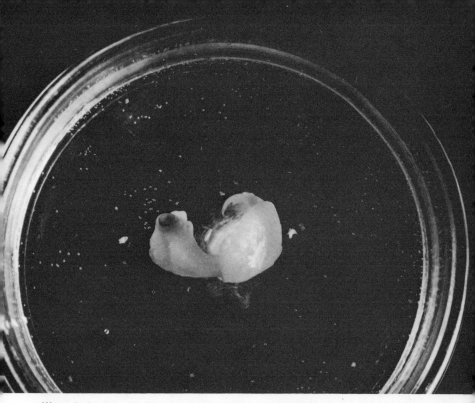

Illus. 8. In this 15-20-mm embryo, note the large head, small cap-like shell and long tail.

The hard parts are all cartilage—the true calcified bone does not appear until after the turtle hatches. Soon the lower shell or *plastron* will catch up with the growth of the embryo and bridges between carapace and plastron will form. A turtle at all stages, from hatching to old age, is heavily dependent upon its eyesight. The eyes and the brain areas that control sight now grow very rapidly and soon appear to be out

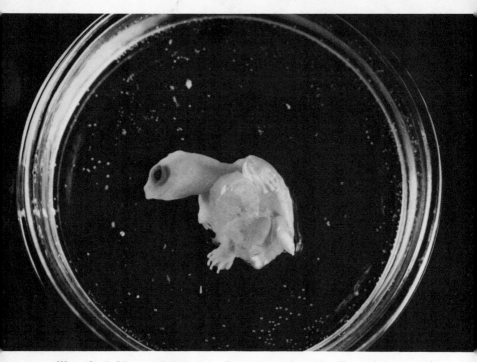

Illus. 9. A 20-mm embryo seen from the under side. Note plastron and fully formed limbs.

of proportion to the rest of the little body. The forefeet and hindfeet are now fully formed and the claws are beginning to appear (Illus. 9).

The carapace contains a bony underlayer called the *plates*, which are made of cartilage that later turns into bone. Above these, most turtles have shields or *scutes* of a tough, flexible material similar to horn. The margins, or *sutures*, of the plates never fall along the

16

Illus. 10. Back and head of a 20-mm embryo. Note fully formed scutes.

same lines as those of the scutes, so the shell is very rigid and strong. This construction is called *lamination* and has many of the properties of man-made plywood. The higher the curve or pitch of a turtle's shell, the stronger it is. The scutes and pitch can be seen well in the later stages of the embryo (Illus. 10).

Now the embryo begins to move and the nerves start to take on their functions. The limbs begin to

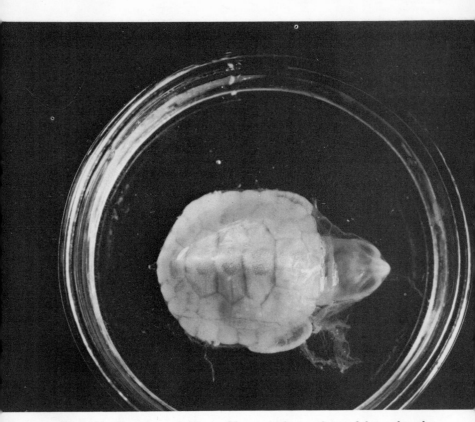

Illus. 11. Top view of 25- to 30-mm embryo, shows faint coloration patterns on the scutes and the embryonic membrane covering the embryo.

take on coloration and the lower shell or plastron hardens. The upper shell, or carapace, has now grown over the limbs completely and the small turtle is a fully formed replica of the adult. The remains of the embryonic membranes still enshroud the whole turtle

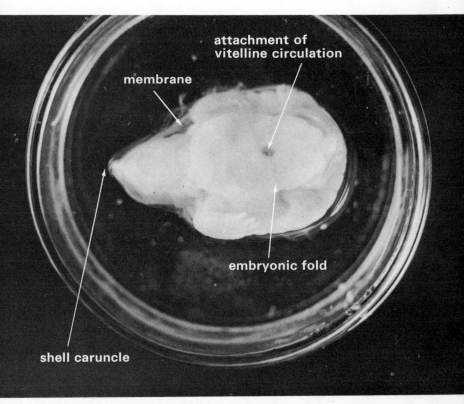

attachment of
vitelline circulation

membrane

embryonic fold

shell caruncle

Illus. 12. In this underside view of a 25- to 30-mm embryo, plastron has the central space where vitalline veins pass through the shell to carry yolk to the embryo. The small knob on the pointed snout is the shell caruncle, which will be used to break a hole in the shell.

(Illus. 11) and a sharp horny knob develops on the end of the beak-like upper jaw (Illus. 11 and 12).

The vitelline circulation still carries the all-important foodstuff from the yolk sac to the young turtle. The embryo lies in a sort of arched or bent position with

Illus. 13. This active hatchling turtle is in the 40-mm stage. Note bright pattern of coloration.

the carapace against the outer and upper part of the eggshell and the plastron slightly bent, with an indistinct fold line across from side to side. This fold straightens out quickly when the embryo hatches as a baby turtle. The plastron, like the carapace, quickly hardens as calcium deposits make the plates bony (Illus. 13).

The hatchling uses the knob, called a *shell caruncle*, to force a hole through the somewhat elastic eggshell and tear an exit slot big enough for its escape. Many

Illus. 14. In a young red-eared turtle, the markings through the head and eye help to break up its silhouette. Its broken pattern, called protective coloration, helps it blend into the pond vegetation where it thrives.

predators catch and eat the young at the critical time when they are leaving the sand-holes and earth-hills where they developed in the eggs and are making their way to water or the woods to hide, feed, and grow. However, many species are provided with protective coloration and are soon lost in their surroundings (Illus. 14). Such species are termed *cryptozoic*, meaning "hidden life," and are rarely seen by man.

Illus. 15. A half-grown Western painted turtle, a very rapid swimmer and strong walker, spends most of its life in ponds and lakes.

The young turtle continues to grow for from three to ten years, depending upon the species. The most extensive growth appears to take place during the first two years. If there is an early spring and a good supply of food, then the young turtles grow quickly during their first summer. Turtles hatched in such years are the largest of their species. However, if there is a cool spring with an early frost, which drives the hatchlings into their first hibernation early, then they never recover the lost growth in later years.

Although everyone thinks of the slow-moving, cumbersome turtle as typical, the half-grown turtles of some species can move quite rapidly on land and swim speedily in water. An especially lively variety is the Western painted turtle of the United States (Illus. 15). Occasionally, the young of this and similar species are sold in pet shops. Few people realize that, if properly fed, these "pets" can grow to nearly a foot in length and weigh several pounds.

ANATOMY OF TURTLES

The anatomy of the turtle is organized in relation to the "box" in which the animal lives. The Southern slider, which has all the regular turtle characteristics, is a good subject for study (Illus. 16). This species spends most of its life in the water except to sun itself and to lay eggs. Like all of the *Cryptodira*, the slider pulls its head straight back into its shell, by forming its neck into an "S" curve (Illus. 17 and 18).

Very few turtles can close up their shell completely and many old and well fed specimens must make the choice of pulling in their head or their tail as both cannot be accommodated in the small space within. Not only are turtles prepared for defence, but most have sharp front claws with which they can tear at an enemy. Most of the turtles eaten in nature fall prey to much larger animals while they are still hatchlings.

Respiratory System

If we open a turtle's shell carefully from the bottom, we can observe a large number of thin muscles covering the internal organs and lying just under the skin of the shoulders and neck. These are the breathing muscles

Illus. 16. A large, old turtle with a grooved shell, in this case a specimen of the Southern slider turtle, one of the largest of American pond turtles.

Illus. 17. A typical cryptodiran, the Southern slider, pulls its head straight back into the shell. The neck forms an "S" pressing against the carapace.

Illus. 18. The turtle's head is completely withdrawn. However, this species cannot close up its shell and must fight sometimes when under attack.

of the turtle. For centuries, naturalists wondered how the turtle could breathe. Some thought that it pumped its head or legs in and out like a bellows, others that it absorbed oxygen through its skin, or perhaps breathed like a fish.

It was finally discovered that turtles breathe by expanding and collapsing their lungs, which lie between their shoulders and their shells (Illus. 19). In most

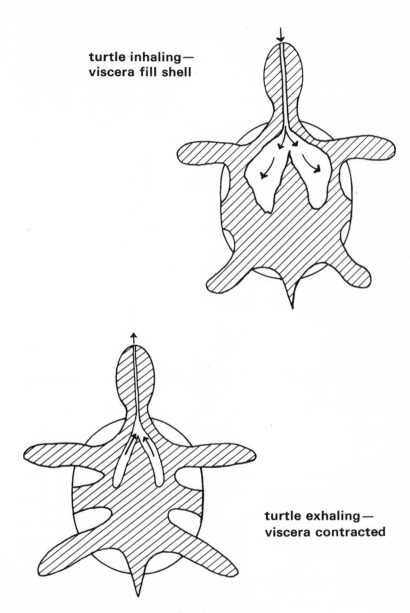

turtle inhaling—
viscera fill shell

turtle exhaling—
viscera contracted

Illus. 19. Respiratory system.

other animals the lungs are situated in front of the other internal organs (viscera) and expand upwards and outwards, away from the backbone. The turtle pulls in all its viscera and certain limb muscles when it exhales and reverses the process, pressing the viscera against the lungs to draw the air into its mouth.

Some species of aquatic turtles can absorb additional oxygen through the lining of the large intestine and cloaca. This is a sort of *rectal* or *anal respiration* practiced by some fishes also. It enables certain aquatic turtles to stay underwater for hours in times of stress.

The general internal anatomy is seen in Illus. 20. The

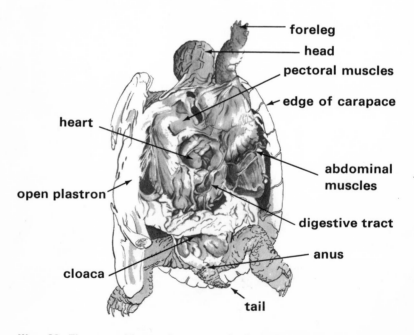

Illus. 20. The general internal anatomy of a large female Southern slider.

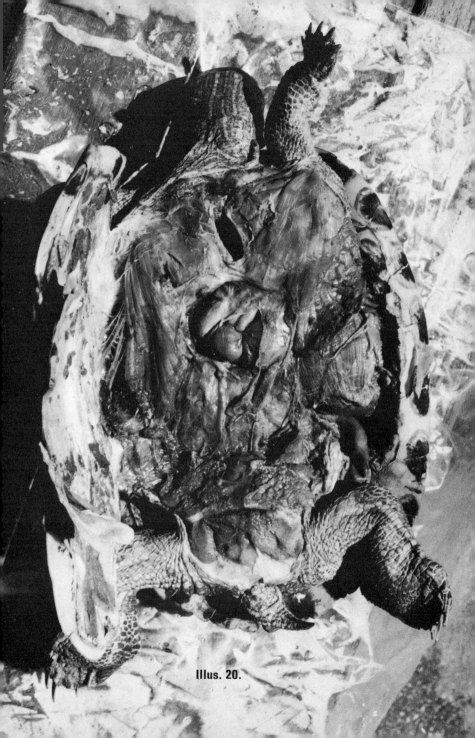

Illus. 20.

Illus. 21. The straight-legged walk of a large tortoise.

shortness and squatness of the turtle's body can be seen in the position of the heart, which is nearly in the middle of the body. This is only a moderately efficient pumping mechanism and is one of the factors in the turtle's low metabolism and cold-bloodedness. The limbs are projected ahead or in back of the plastron and work something like oars. Notice the straight, stiff gait of the great Galápagos tortoise, weighing some 500 pounds (Illus. 21).

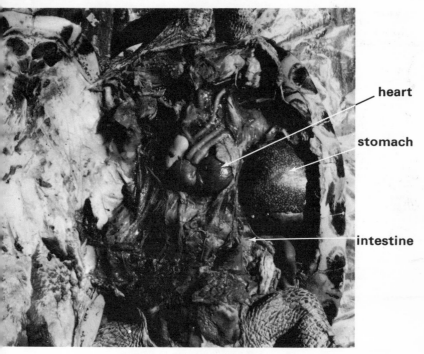

heart

stomach

intestine

Illus. 22. The digestive system of a turtle.

Digestive System

The digestive system of tortoises and turtles (Illus. 22) is typical of reptiles. Since the tortoise has no teeth, it must break up and digest its food completely in its stomach. There is some evidence that certain species swallow (ingest) gravel or small stones to aid the grinding action of the powerful stomach walls.

Illus. 23. Eggs at all degrees of maturity removed from a large female turtle.

Most food is ingested whole or torn off in pieces and swallowed. The tortoise's and turtle's digestive tract is not overly long, as is the case with many plant-eating animals. It is thought by some experts that all turtles are omnivorous, that they will eat both animal and plant material, although each species undoubtedly has its preferences. The digestive system is supplied with specialized enzymes from several glands that are unique to reptiles.

The thickly walled digestive tract ends in a *cloaca* where both solid and semi-liquid nitrogenous waste products are collected and expelled (voided).

Egg Development

The eggs are formed in the body of the female in a series of involved tubes. Yolk, albumen and the eggshell are added as the egg develops. Most species lay groups (called clutches) of from 3 to 20 eggs (Illus. 23). However, the small Tornier's tortoise lays only one egg, while the giant leatherback sea turtle may lay several hundred. The tropical sea and river turtles often lay several clutches per year and the same is true of some of the pond turtles of the southern United States.

Since all the eggs which a female has to develop and lay for years, if not for a lifetime, are present in different stages of development inside her body, large sea tortoises are often killed by man for their eggs which are edible. Such slaughter by man has brought a number of tortoise species to the brink of extinction. Turtles assure the future of their species, not by caring for and guarding their young, but by producing enough eggs and depositing them in enough different places that by sheer probability some will survive. Studies made of turtle populations show that destruction of the large majority of young hatchlings is not as disastrous to the species as catching and killing the mature females. In Illus. 23 the eggs of one Southern slider female are seen in the egg membrane, and there are nearly 50 in this one specimen. Nearly 2,000 such eggs were found in one female sea turtle.

After mating, the female turtle has a sac for storing male sperm. Thus a female turtle can continue to lay fertile eggs up to four years after mating. However, the potency of the sperm is lowered each year after the first, and greater infertility of the eggs results.

All turtles, when depositing their eggs, use their back feet to cover up the clutch with sand or earth.

Circulatory System

The circulatory system of the turtle (Illus. 24) is compact and regular, and it works well with the turtle's low blood volume and slow metabolic rate. While an individual blood cell may survive only a few weeks in man, laboratory tests have shown blood cells to last up to 800 days in turtles! The complete vascular system of the turtle, with the spongy network of the lungs branching off at either side of the heart, is shown in Illus. 25. The blood supply in the female is more extensive around the lower visceral region because of the need to nourish the eggs.

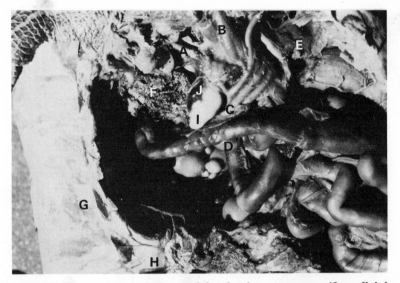

Illus. 24. The anatomy of the turtle's circulatory system. (Superficial muscles have been removed.)

A. carotid artery   B. trachea   C. aortic arch

D. gall bladder   E. lungs   F. lobe of the liver

G. plastron   H. carapace   I. ventricle   J. auricle

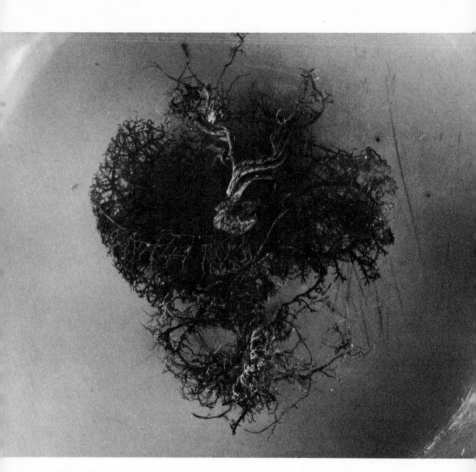

Illus. 25. The venous and arterial system of a large turtle. (Heart is in the middle.)

AGE OF TURTLES

The shields on a turtle's shell grow throughout life and add small concentric rings with each growth period. Although, under certain conditions, these can be counted and used like the rings of trees to compute the turtle's age, the method is not reliable. More accurate are the estimates based on the number of grooves and nicks which are always characteristic of an old specimen (Illus. 26). Some tropical turtles have shells which decay along the ridges, and sustain moulds and green algae which provide very good natural camouflage (Illus. 27).

The longevity of turtles is legendary. In all too many cases great ages are ascribed to turtles that cannot be scientifically proven. However, it seems likely that most turtles can survive up to 30 or 40 years. Needless to say, there are some magnificent exceptions. The 18th-century French explorer, Marion de Fresne, captured a giant Aldabra tortoise (Illus. 28) in the Seychelles Islands of the Indian Ocean in the year 1766. Full-grown at capture, it died on the

Illus. 26. An old campaigner suns his well worn carapace.

Illus. 27. A tropical fresh-water turtle covered with ridges, bumps, and holes, all coated with fungus and algae.

Illus. 28. A mature Aldabra tortoise, native to a small group of islands in the Indian Ocean. This specimen is one of the longest-lived of all vertebrates—it lived more than 152 years.

island of Mauritius after a fatal fall in 1918. After reaching maturity, this great animal had lived 152 years!

It is scientifically established that box tortoises have lived as long as 80 years. In 1905, a young alligator snapping turtle was presented to the Philadelphia

Illus. 29. This old fellow is at least 68 if not 70 years of age or more. A magnificent specimen of the alligator snapping turtle, it was sent to the Philadelphia Aquarium in 1905.

Aquarium. Years later the same reptile was given to the Philadelphia Zoological Garden, America's first zoo. In 1973, he was still going strong, in a newly rebuilt tank. This gigantic fresh-water turtle now weighs nearly 200 pounds and is at least 68 years of age (Illus. 29). Other specimens have reached 75 years in captivity.

It is known that at one time, at least up until the late 18th century, sea turtles of immense size and doubtless great age were occasionally captured from sailing vessels. Now that the seas of the world are plied by modern ships and steel weapons and tools are available to persons living in the tropics, these monsters have been destroyed. Some sea turtles still weigh up to a half ton, but the century-old specimens of a ton or more have probably all perished.

Turtles continue to grow slowly even after reaching sexual maturity. But giants within a species, that is specimens half again bigger than their common relatives, are very rare. It appears that the smaller pond turtles do not live as long as the larger land-dwelling forms.

KINDS OF TURTLES
AND TORTOISES

Box Tortoises

One of the most fascinating and interesting of the land turtles is the common box tortoise, found throughout much of Canada, the United States and Mexico. It has two special features which distinguish it from most other turtles—a high-pitched, rounded shell and a hinge which permits it to enclose its head completely inside the box. There is a characteristic sprinkle of yellow markings over the shell, also (Illus. 30).

There are literally dozens of sub-groupings and coloration patterns among box tortoises. In fact, the pattern on the plastron is quite individual, with no two box tortoises having exactly the same markings and coloration (Illus. 31). There are also substantial differences in the brightness of the pattern, especially between male and female (Illus. 32). Also, the male

Illus. 30. The heavy, high-pitched shell marked with keeled scutes, hides the box tortoise on the forest floor.

Illus. 31. The box tortoise's hinge across the plastron and the characteristically different color patterns in two mature adults.

Illus. 32. Two adult box tortoises—the duller female to the left, the brighter male to the right.

plastron is usually slightly concave, while the female plastron is convex (Illus. 33).

The young of the box tortoise hide under forest leaves and dead plant material until after their first year. This is one key to the survival of so many box tortoises in almost every rural area (Illus. 34). Other assets are keen eyesight, and a strong beak well adapted for the crushing of beetles and snails, as well as for

Illus. 33. The plastron of the male (right) has a slight hollow depression, or concavity, while the female (left) has a slight rounding, or convexity, between hinge and tail.

Illus. 34. A large adult box tortoise in its forest home; to its right is a hatchling. The hatchlings are very secretive for the first year and are rarely seen.

Illus. 35. The bright eye and bird-like beak of the Carolina box tortoise. These land turtles have good eyesight and can distinguish coloration.

plucking berries (Illus. 35). Like other tortoises, this species senses vibrations through the ground and thus has warning of approaching danger in time to hide.

The box tortoise is a poor swimmer, preferring merely to wade along the bank of a stream or pond. It derives considerable moisture from its food, and is particularly fond of low growing fruits such as the wild strawberry, the gooseberry and blackberry. Its clawed forefeet (Illus. 36) are better equipped for digging than for swimming, and this land turtle can dig down rather swiftly in loose soil which it must do

Illus. 36. The forepaw of the Carolina box turtle. Long claws help in feeding and mating and are especially adapted for digging.

to escape the frost line in the northern part of its range. In southern Ontario, box tortoises have been found wintering four feet or more below ground level. The hind feet (Illus. 37) are very well adapted for traction on either the forest floor or on meadow grasses.

The box tortoise does well in captivity if provided with an outdoor pen in summer of no less than 20 square feet and given a place to hide from the hot sun; a small tree or bush is excellent. After a few weeks in captivity without undue poking or pestering, the

Illus. 37. The powerful hind paw with its curved traction claws for travelling overland.

more aggressive specimens will learn to feed from your fingers. It is a good idea, if possible, to release captive turtles into their natural habitat in the late summer so that they can provide for their own hibernation. Carrying over hibernating animals in captivity is a tricky business best left to zoos and other animal refuges.

The two biggest enemies of the box tortoise are the inexperienced collector, who allows them to starve to death, and the motor-car which yearly crushes countless numbers of these appealing animals on the highway.

Illus. 38. The bright Eastern painted turtle catches the afternoon sun on a rock.

The Painted Turtle

There are many interesting adaptations among aquatic turtles. One of the most widely distributed in the United States is the painted turtle, often seen by fresh-water fishermen (Illus. 38). It is not merely one of the most brightly marked of all turtles, it is also a very strong swimmer spending nearly its entire life in the water. Yet, when it does come on dry land, it is a fast walker! On occasion its numbers will be so plentiful as to seriously deplete the supply of shellfish and arthropods on which it feeds. This turtle swims fast enough to catch small fish which it devours with

Illus. 39. The painted turtle is extremely fast and can disappear rapidly, like this old male diving off his sunning rock.

relish and agility. Even at the slightest hint of a shadow or vibration, the painted turtle will head for deep water (Illus. 39).

It makes a good pet but must be kept in fairly deep water, at least two feet, with suitable sunning spots. Water turtles need fairly clean water, although some varieties can survive in stagnant ponds, chiefly the snappers.

One easy way to keep turtle tanks clean is to feed the turtles in a sink or tank with a drain and keep them in roomy living quarters. The mess of feeding and their wastes can then be kept out of their residence tank.

Illus. 40. The skull-like shell of the musk turtle. This ferocious reptile lives on the bottom of mud-bound streams.

The Musk Turtle

A common and interesting turtle of the mud flats and marshes is the musk, or stinkpot, turtle. Small, and of a dark muddy brown hue, this turtle and its near relatives range all the way from New England, west to the Mississippi Valley and south to Latin America (Illus. 40). Once in a while, it may be seen sunning in streams, but with only the top of the carapace sticking above the water. It has a long neck and rapid movements and is very quick to snap at anything

Illus. 41. The withdrawn head of a musk turtle. It cannot close its shell and will fight if provoked.

which comes near it. It is related to the snapping turtles and, like them, rarely leaves the water (Illus. 41). It has the front protruding nostrils and bad temper that mark many bottom-dwelling aquatic turtles (Illus. 42).

Like other fresh-water turtles, which hide on the bottom of streams, the plastron of the musk turtle is reduced and the bridges actually extend inward across

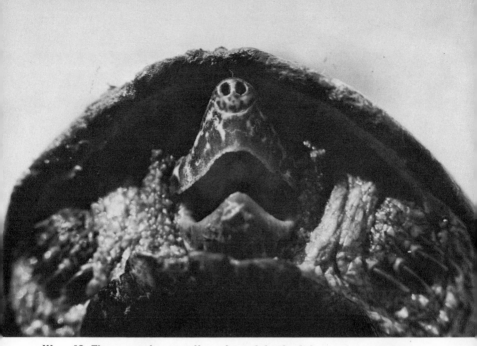

Illus. 42. The protrusive nostrils and rough beak of the musk turtle. Since its shell will not close, this is its defensive position.

the plastron, to hold it in place. The head can be retracted until only the fore part of the tough skull shows, and the legs and tail are tucked up under the much larger, knobby carapace (Illus. 43). This is one of the smallest turtles, only reaching 4 inches at maturity and laying small clutches of eggs, which can easily be confused with those of snakes and lizards.

Illus. 43. The plastron of the musk turtle is sufficiently smaller than the carapace to allow the legs to be tucked in under the upper shell.

These turtles can climb well with their sharp claws. Sometimes they climb far out on low branches overhanging a stream to sun themselves, and have been known to fall down into boats or onto fishermen. Here, then, is a tree-climbing turtle!

Illus. 44. The finely marked head of the diamondback terrapin.

The Diamondback Terrapin

Along the salt-water beaches and causeways of eastern North America, the diamondback terrapin is common. A handsome animal esteemed for its edible flesh, the tribe has been reduced in number by terrapin hunters. It is at home in both fresh and salt water and will lay eggs readily in captivity. An over-all light grey shade with darker markings is characteristic of the coloration of this species, as is the unique pattern of diamond-shaped shields of the shell (Illus. 44). The

Illus. 45. The terrapin, a gourmet's delight, has watchful eyes.

female may grow to a foot in length, the males somewhat less.

This is a species at home on land or in the water (Illus. 46). However, it is usually found in brackish water from New England to the Texas coast. The carapace is usually very strong and heavy—this is a powerful animal for its size, and like the painted turtles,

Illus. 46. A medium-sized female diamondback.

it is a strong swimmer. The plastron is large, nearly flat, and has a very pleasing pattern (Illus. 47). These turtles eat all manner of seafood, including shrimps, and become reasonably good pets. However, they often catch two of the most common diseases of turtles in captivity, soft-shell, a dietary deficiency, and fungus.

Unfortunately, the diamondback has a liking for wandering out of the water at night and seems to follow bright lights such as those on causeways and bridges over shallow water. The results are devastating,

Illus. 47. The flat plastron of the diamondback.

with as many as 100 terrapins a mile being killed by motor vehicles.

Snapping Turtles

The snapping turtles, widely famed in song and story, are often credited with powers they do not possess. Contrary to folklore, they cannot shear off a swimmer's feet, snap a broomstick in their jaws, or chase dogs. The most widely dispersed of these tortoises is the common, or Northern, snapper (Illus. 48). The shell is well rounded and the forefeet are very strong

Illus. 48. The Northern snapper, with strong forelegs and reduced shell, makes its way across a tidal flat.

(Illus. 49). The old veteran often has a well scarred shell from many mating battles (Illus. 50). The wrinkled skin and the scaly plates on the tail are typical features of this animal (Illus. 51).

The special adaptations of the snapper are many. It is fitted with very strong fore claws (Illus. 52) and hooked hind claws (Illus. 53). These animals are quite

Illus. 49. This old snapper sitting on a low stump looks almost like a rock.

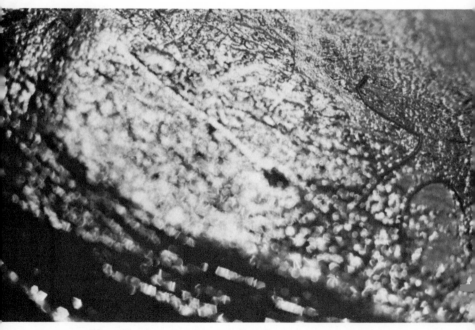

Illus. 50. The strongly gouged shell of an old female snapper.

Illus. 51. The snapper's elephant-like tail plates remind one of a dinosaur.

Illus. 52. Fore claws of a common snapper.

Illus. 53. Long hind claws of snapper.

Illus. 54. A large snapper shows the length and muscles of its neck, while flipping itself over.

Illus. 55. Fighting stance of a snapper.

heavy, often weighing 10 pounds and more. The neck is long (Illus. 54). They rarely try to hide in their shells, but will stand their ground when provoked (Illus. 55). In small towns in the country they often walk along the drainage ditches after a period of rain. The eyes are well hidden (Illus. 56) by protective coloration—this species relies heavily on its keen eyesight, sometimes lying motionless beneath the water until an unsuspecting prey comes into range.

In their marshy homes, these tortoises stay very close to the surface of the water, waiting for victims.

Illus. 56. Snapper eye and orbit (area surrounding eye).

They will eat almost any animal. The author once kept a large common snapper in a 50-gallon tank in his back yard in North Carolina. On various occasions it pulled in and drowned birds, and once killed a squirrel. It would attempt to eat nearly anything, but was especially voracious when eating ground beef or horsemeat. All snappers are fond of earthworms and small fish, which they usually swallow whole. They will become finger-tame but at some risk to the finger—they are capable of giving a nasty pinch and breaking the skin.

Illus. 57. This young alligator snapper still possesses its egg caruncle and sharp beak.

The Alligator Snapper

The alligator snapper is one of the most feared tortoises. It makes its home in the Mississippi Valley and the region about the Gulf of Mexico. One specimen weighed in excess of 200 pounds, making it the largest of fresh-water turtles. The young are exact miniatures of the adult, possessing the same horny, ridged shell, sharp beak and wrinkled skin (Illus. 57).

Illus. 58. Reduced carapace of the alligator snapper.

Illus. 59. The sharp eyes and protruding nose of a juvenile alligator snapping turtle.

Illus. 60. The alligator snapper has an unusually long tail.

The carapace is reduced to a great extent as is typical with the heavier water turtles (Illus. 58). The carapace never conceals the greatly enlarged head. These turtles cannot fully retract their heads as they have necks substantially as long as their shells and develop very rapidly. As juveniles they have sharp eyesight (Illus. 59). They are especially adapted for life on the bottom of ponds. One unique appendage is the rather long tail (Illus. 60). As in the related musk turtles, the plastron is very much reduced and barely covers the underside of the turtle (Illus. 61).

Illus. 61. The heavy legs and reduced plastron of the alligator snapper.

Old snappers grow to large sizes and great ages—
some have lived 75 years or more—and the carapace
ridges grow extensively (Illus. 62). Mature snappers
stay motionless on the bottom of the stream or pond
with their large mouths open. The inside of the mouth
is usually a soft pink. In the middle is a worm-like

Illus. 62. A 68-year-old snapper with a deeply ridged shell.

appendage on the tongue which attracts fish into the massive jaws, where they are then swallowed.

Many smaller turtles are gregarious, that is, they gather in large groups. If there is a lack of space on the rocks, fallen trees or other prominences upon which they climb for sunning, they will climb on each other

Illus. 63. Gregarious turtles often climb on each other to sun themselves.

(Illus. 63). The big snappers, too, may often be seen doing the very same thing!

The Chicken and Soft-Shell Turtles

Two other water tortoises have interesting adaptations. The chicken turtle has an especially long neck, with which it can raise its head and breathe from the bottom of a ditch or pond, or can stretch it quite far out to feed. This animal, of which there are several

Illus. 64. Two chicken turtles, one with its head extended in the typical slight "S" curve.

species, has yellow stripes on its long neck and stripes on its forelegs. Chicken turtles were once sold for food in markets and may have gotten the name by reason of their tender meat. They are Pleurodira, and the neck is more often than not carried in a sort of shallow "S" curve (Illus. 64).

Widely distributed in Asia, Africa and North America are the soft-shell turtles of which there are numerous species. These have no shields covering

Illus. 65. A juvenile soft-shell turtle showing the flat carapace, long head and tube snout of the species.

the plates of the carapace, but only a leathery skin which ends in a sort of fringe at the back of the carapace. The head is elongated and the protrusive snout is almost a tube. These turtles are very ill-tempered and grow quite large, two feet in their natural habitats (Illus. 65). Many are brightly patterned and are sometimes kept as pets, in spite of their tendency to bite.

Illus. 66. The strange grin of the matamata, one of the world's ugliest animals.

The Matamata

Of all the turtles in the world, one of the strangest is the matamata, a water turtle of the Guianas and northern Brazil. This animal is covered with all sorts of fleshy protuberances and has a great leering mouth and tiny beady eyes (Illus. 66). The head, when

Illus. 67. The profile of the matamata.

viewed from the side, reveals a long, tubular nose
(Illus. 67) with tiny pink nostrils, a mouth which
spreads well around and back of the eyes and head,
(Illus. 68), and a very wide neck. All about the mouth
and on the lower jaw are wrinkles and deep hanging
strips of skin. The eyes are very sharp and, like most
turtles, the matamata senses vibrations rather than hears
sounds. A member of the Pleurodira, it wraps its
muscular neck under its hard and heavy shell. So ugly
are these creatures that Latin Americans often refer
to an unattractive person as having the face of a matamata.

Illus. 68. The immense mouth of the matamata.

The lumpy carapace develops holes and is often covered with fungi or algae (Illus. 69). The reduced plastron, similar to that of the alligator snapping turtle, and the thick muscle-bound neck can best be seen from beneath (Illus. 70). These turtles wait for fish to be attracted to their wiggling and waving skin flaps. Then they expand their neck with a great deal of force and literally suck their prey into the mouth. After the fish is caught they expel the excess water. They eat voraciously in captivity and live in zoos for many years.

Illus. 69. The ridged matamata carapace.

Illus. 70. When the matamata is on its back, you can see its wide neck
(lower right).

Illus. 71. The plateless turtle, a very attractive species now close to extinction.

The New Guinea Plateless Turtle

Sad to say, many of the fresh-water turtles are on the brink of extinction. The World Wildlife Fund has placed the medium-sized New Guinea plateless turtle high on the list of threatened species. Like the soft-shell turtle, it has no shields, only a skin covering the bone plates. It has limbs resembling those of the sea turtles, and a long protruding nose (Illus. 71).

These turtles were once found in abundance in the Fly River region of southern New Guinea and in parts of Indonesia, but they have long been used by the local people for food, with the result that much of their breeding ground has been destroyed. The mature turtles are little more than a foot long, but they are superb swimmers and are in continual motion, except for brief rest periods on the bottom.

Sea Turtles

Most of the world is covered with water and the seas once abounded with huge turtles. In marine turtles, the fore limbs are modified into flippers. The animals live almost their entire lives in the sea, except when the females crawl ashore to lay their eggs on the beach. When the eggs hatch, the tiny turtles scramble frantically for the protection of the sea, seeking to escape the predatory sea birds waiting for them along the beach.

Unfortunately, these great reptiles, many of which once grew to more than a ton in weight, are now facing extinction, too. The hawksbill turtle has been pursued and killed relentlessly for its carapace, the tortoise-shell, so valuable in commerce. Another species, the green turtle, is hunted for its flesh, the basic ingredient of turtle soup. The green turtle is one

Illus. 72. A green turtle gulping down a squid.

of the most active. A fast-swimming green turtle of about 40 pounds weight is pursuing a squid for breakfast in Illus. 72.

Marine turtles usually have much reduced shells, and in one species, the leatherback, the bony plates are reduced to mere discs. The leatherback, also called the luth and the leathery turtle, is so different from all other chelonians in the structure of its carapace, that zoologists put it in a group of its own.

Illus. 73. A large loggerhead excavating a hole with its hind feet.

On rare occasions, great sea turtles will come ashore to lay their eggs in very unexpected places. The Atlantic loggerhead, for example, rarely spawns as far north as central Florida. In early July, 1972, a boy at the resort of Ocean City, New Jersey, spotted a medium-sized loggerhead lumbering up on the beach in what would be by mid-morning a very crowded area. The police kept the crowd away while the great beast

Illus. 74. A crowd of well-wishers and a police guard arrive.

excavated a hole and deposited well over 100 eggs. Detective Paul Counsellor took a series of photographs of the egg-laying and return of the turtle to the sea (Illus. 73–78). The Philadelphia Zoo removed the eggs to an incubator for hatching, and announced plans to release the hatchlings (Illus. 79 and 80), when old enough, to a biological station in the Caribbean.

Illus. 75. The eggs buried, the female begins her heavy journey back to the sea.

Illus. 76. The female turtle slowly inches toward the sea.

Illus. 77. Almost to the water's edge, the loggerhead still has an escort.

Illus. 78. Swimming depth achieved, the turtle soon disappears with powerful strokes.

Illus. 79. The young loggerhead turtle, one of the hatchlings from the eggs removed from the Ocean City Beach.

Loggerhead turtles are carnivorous, as are most turtles. The green turtle, however, is largely a vegetarian, pasturing on the roots of eel-grass. Like that of other herbivorous animals, its flesh is esteemed by man. In the past, vast numbers of green turtles were caught as they came ashore to lay their eggs.

Live green turtles were once kept aboard ships to

Illus. 80. The greatly reduced plastron of the loggerhead turtle. The attachment point of the yolk sac is right between the man's thumb and third finger.

provide a steady supply of fresh meat on long voyages. The green turtle cannot right itself if turned on its back—the poor creatures were kept on their backs in the hold until needed.

Illus. 81. A fully grown Galápagos tortoise showing the deep-set eyes and thick-skulled head.

Giant Land Tortoises

The great and lesser tortoises of arid regions rely on their shells as insulation against excessive heat and often derive their water from the plants upon which they feed. The tortoises which inhabit rocky islands of the tropics are found in two areas far removed, one in the Pacific and the other in the Indian Ocean. The Galápagos tortoise (Illus. 81) has virtually no enemy

Illus. 82. Digging with its long claws, the Galápagos tortoise inches along, foraging for vegetable matter, its chief food.

but man on its barren islands in the Pacific Ocean, about a thousand miles west of Ecuador. These immense tortoises leave tracks in the gravel as they hunt for food (Illus. 82). The expressionless face of the tortoise (Illus. 83) and its slow movements do not reveal its intelligence but land turtles seem to be more intelligent than the aquatic species. Many Galápagos turtles can be tamed and learn to come to a keeper for attention.

Illus. 83. Head of a Galápagos tortoise.

Illus. 84. Two giant Aldabra tortoises.

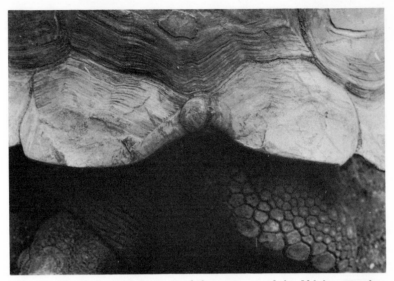

Illus. 85. The neck and front part of the carapace of the Aldabra tortoise, showing the nuchal shield.

The Galápagos and the Indian Ocean Aldabra tortoises (Illus. 84) are often confused but although they look very similar they can be distinguished by the fact that the Aldabra has a protrusion on its carapace just above the neck called a *nuchal* shield (Illus. 85), while the Galápagos has no nuchal shield at that point on the carapace (Illus. 86).

Even though they are now very carefully protected in their native areas, it is not yet known if the Aldabra and Galápagos tortoises will survive. When a population of any animal falls to a small number, in the

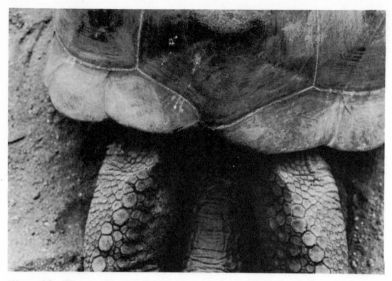

Illus. 86. The neck and front part of the carapace of the Galápagos tortoise, showing the absence of the nuchal shield.

thousands of individuals, any accident of nature can push the species to extinction. It is likely that many turtle species will no longer exist on earth by the year 2000.

THE TURTLE IN NATURE

Most of the world's turtles and tortoises spend their lives in or near water. They derive their food and water needs directly from where they live. They emerge from the water chiefly to sun themselves (Illus. 87). This need has some relationship to the turtle's internal production of vitamin A.

Large bunches of water plants (Illus. 88) make a convenient hiding place for young turtles. The tiny hatchlings (Illus. 89) make a tasty mouthful for herons and other predators. Not every hatchling is camouflaged by its markings—some are albinos (Illus. 90). Albinos occur as often among turtles as among other animals, but few ever survive the hatchling stage, for they are easy marks for predators. Very few turtles live in rapidly flowing water but many live in stagnant and swampy areas (Illus. 91). Here their only enemy is man.

Turtles have filled a niche in nature as predators and scavengers for at least 250,000,000 years. Their place

Illus. 87. An Eastern painted turtle sunning on a log.

Illus. 88. Clumps of water plants provide a hiding place for hatchlings.

Illus. 89. Egg and hatchling of diamondback terrapin.

Illus. 90. Albino hatchling.

Illus. 91. A plant-choked swamp with a seasonal overflow of water is a likely place to find turtles.

in nature and ecology has been encroached upon by first wild and then domestic mammals. We must protect their habitats. If we do not, we shall be responsible for the disappearance of one of the world's most fascinating and distinctive animal groups, and one that is quite harmless to man.

INDEX